HUGHISMS

A LEGACY OF LIFE LESSONS

REGINA PEERY

NATIONAL WHITE-REINHARDT AWARD WINNER

innovo
PUBLISHING.COM

Published by Innovo Publishing, LLC
www.innovopublishing.com
1-888-546-2111

Providing Full-Service Publishing Services for Christian Authors, Artists & Ministries: Hardbacks, Paperbacks, eBooks, Audiobooks, Music, Screenplays & Curricula

HUGHISMS
A LEGACY OF LIFE LESSONS

ISBN: 978-1-61314-772-6

Cover Design & Interior Layout: Innovo Publishing, LLC
Illustrations by: Makayla Peery

Printed in the United States of America
U.S. Printing History
First Edition: 2021

— DEDICATION —

To my dad's students,
who over nearly 40 years brought so much joy to his life and
knew him best through the words,
"Here by the Owl."

My brothers, Nathan and Byron,
both educators of agriculture, farmers, and amazing fathers.

My five beautiful nieces:
Makayla, Janie, Adrianna, Katie, and Libby,
who knew him best as Grandpa or Pa.

My Mom:
a special lady of faith, strength, talent, love, grit & grace
who taught us by example that we can do all things
through Christ who strengthens us.

SPECIAL TRIBUTE TO:

My brother, Marcus,
for often adding joy and laughter to many of the Hughisms
throughout our lives.

All our dedicated farmers,
who are working hard today to improve on yesterday
and to provide a better tomorrow
for us all.

AUTHOR'S INTRODUCTION

Hugh "Sonny" Ervin Peery was a veteran, a farmer, and a teacher. In my eyes and heart, he was the daddy that was made just for me. Through his words of wisdom, humor, and encouragement, he taught me about life.

I hope, in some way, the Hughisms in this book will help you along life's journey–wherever your travels may lead.

Please take from these pages whatever it is that your heart may need–joy, hope, encouragement, comfort, guidance, laughter, or love–and pass it on.

With much love,

Regina

THE HARDEST PART
IS GETTING STARTED.

Brothers and sisters, I do not consider myself yet to have taken hold of it. But one thing I do: Forgetting what is behind and straining toward what is ahead, I press on toward the goal to win the prize for which God has called me heavenward in Christ Jesus.

—Philippians 3:13-14

DON'T BE A LOST BALL
IN TALL WEEDS.

Trust in the Lord with all your heart and lean not on your own understanding.

—Proverbs 3:5

I NEED TO SEE
YOUR EYES.

I am the vine; you are the branches. If you remain in me and I in you, you will bear much fruit; apart from me you can do nothing.

—John 15:5

LET ME SAY THIS
ABOUT THAT.

"For I know the plans I have for you," declares the Lord, "plans to prosper you and not to harm you, plans to give you a hope and a future."

—Jeremiah 29:11

THE EASY WAY
IS NOT ALWAYS THE SMARTEST WAY.

Whatever you do, work at it with all your heart, as working for the Lord, not for human masters, since you know that you will receive an inheritance from the Lord as a reward. It is the Lord Christ you are serving.

—Colossians 3:23-24

YOU CAN WORK A LOT
OF LIFE'S PROBLEMS OUT BY WATCHING A FIRE.

Be still and know that I am God; I will be exalted among the nations, I will be exalted in the earth.

—Psalm 46:10

SOMEONE ALWAYS HAS IT
WORSE THAN YOU DO.

Yet what we suffer now is nothing compared to the glory he will reveal to us later.

—Romans 8:18

ALWAYS FIND SOMETHING
TO LAUGH ABOUT.

A joyful heart is good medicine, but a crushed spirit dries up the bones.

—Proverbs 17:22

"Don't worry, Grandpa. We're safe as long as we keep standing on your tractor."

TAKE CARE OF YOURSELF.
IF YOU DON'T, YOU CAN'T TAKE CARE OF ANYONE ELSE.

Come to me, all you who are weary and burdened, and I will give you rest.

—Matthew 11:28

AN EGG HAS EVERYTHING
YOU NEED IN IT.

It is not good to eat too much honey, nor is it honorable to search out matters that are too deep.

—Proverbs 25:27

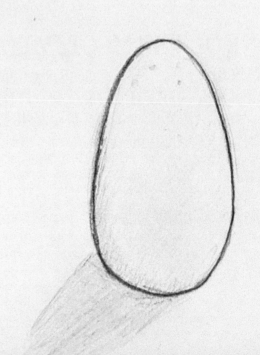

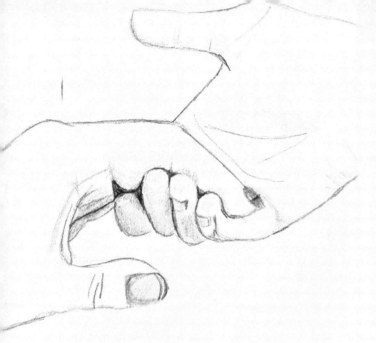

WHEN SOMEONE NEEDS
A HELPING HAND, GIVE THEM YOURS.

For I was hungry and you gave me food. I was thirsty and you gave me a drink. I was a stranger and you welcomed me. I was naked and you clothed me. I was sick and you visited me. . . . Truly, I say to you, as you did it to one of the least of these my brothers, you did it for me.

—Matthew 25:35-40

ONE OF THE MOST IMPORTANT
WORDS IN THE ENGLISH LANGUAGE IS THE WORD *WE*. ONE OF THE LEAST IMPORTANT IS THE WORD *I*.

As iron sharpens iron, so one person sharpens another.

—Proverbs 27:17

TIP YOUR HAT

TO THE PERSON SITTING HIGH ON THE TRACTOR & THE PERSON WADING IN THE DITCH WITH THE SAME NOD OF RESPECT.

For by the grace given me I say to every one of you: Do not think of yourself more highly than you ought, but rather think of yourself with sober judgment, in accordance with the faith God has distributed to each of you.

—Romans 12:3

YOU CAN COUNT
YOUR TRUE FRIENDS ON ONE HAND.

Greater love has no one than this: to lay down one's life for one's friends.

—John 15:13

YOU AND ME ARE...
TWO AND TWO!

And the very hairs on your head are all numbered. So don't be afraid; you are more valuable to God than a flock of sparrows.

—Luke 12:7

ALWAYS TAKE TIME
TO GO WHERE TIME DOESN'T MATTER.

Whoever dwells in the shelter of the Most High will rest in the shadow of the Almighty.

—Psalm 91:1

A HAYFIELD IS
A BEAUTIFUL THING GOD GAVE US.

In the beginning God created the heavens and the earth.

—Genesis 1:1

WAVE WITH YOUR
WHOLE ARM.

The joy of the Lord is my strength.

—Nehemiah 8:10

WHEN YOU SMILE,

MAKE SURE YOU SHOW YOUR TEETH.

The Lord has done GREAT things for us and we are filled with joy.

—Psalm 126:3

YOUR WEEK WILL

GO MUCH BETTER WITH A FRIED PIE.

Delight yourself also in the Lord; and He shall give you the desires of your heart.

—Psalm 37:4

EVERY DAY IS

NOT GOING TO BE A GOOD DAY, BUT IT WILL BE THE GOOD DAYS THAT HELP YOU GET THROUGH THE BAD.

Have I not commanded you? Be strong and courageous. Do not be afraid; do not be discouraged, for the LORD your God will be with you wherever you go.

—Joshua 1:9

YOU CAN VISIT THERE—

BUT YOU CAN'T STAY THERE.

Weeping may endure for a night, but joy comes in the morning.

—Psalm 30:5

THIS TOO...
SHALL PASS.

For everything there is a season, and a time for everything, and a season for every activity under the heavens; a time to be born and a time to die, a time to plant and a time to uproot, a time to kill and a time to heal, a time to tear down and time to build, a time to weep and a time to laugh, a time to mourn and a time to dance, a time to scatter stones and a time to gather them, a time to embrace and a time to refrain from embracing, a time to search and a time to give up, a time to keep and a time to throw away, a time to tear and a time to mend, a time to be silent and a time to speak, a time to love and a time to hate, a time for war and a time for peace.

—Ecclesiastes 3:1-8

PEOPLE ARE ALWAYS
GOING TO HAVE SOMETHING TO SAY. IT'S THE THINGS YOU SAY TO YOURSELF THAT REALLY MATTER.

You, dear children, are from God and have overcome them, because the one who is in you is greater than the one who is in the world.

—1 John 4:4

BEING ENVIOUS OF SOMEONE

ISN'T BECOMING. BESIDES...YOU DON'T KNOW HOW MUCH SOMEONE OWNS & HOW MUCH SOMEONE OWES.

Every good and perfect gift is from above, coming down from the Father of the heavenly lights, who does not change like shifting shadows.

—James 1:17

OTHERS CAN BRAG

ON YOU, AND YOU CAN BRAG ON OTHERS. BUT, NO ONE WANTS TO HEAR YOU BOAST ABOUT YOURSELF.

Do you see a man who is wise in his own eyes? There is more hope for a fool than for him.

—Proverbs 26:12

ALWAYS BE ABLE
TO LOOK THE PERSON IN THE MIRROR IN THE EYES.

Let your eyes look straight ahead; fix your gaze directly before you. Give careful thought to the paths for your feet and be steadfast in all your ways. Do not turn to the right or the left; keep your foot from evil.

—Proverbs 4:25-27

YOU'RE TOUGH...
AIN'T YA, GIRL?

I can do all things through Christ who strengthens me.

—Philippians 4:13

IF YOU ARE GOING TO ASK

GOD FOR A SAFE TRIP, DON'T FORGET TO THANK HIM – WHEN HE GIVES YOU ONE.

Give thanks to the Lord, for He is good; His love endures forever.

—1 Chronicles 16:34

YOU CAN WORRY

YOURSELF TO DEATH ABOUT THINGS THAT MAY NEVER HAPPEN.

Be anxious about nothing, but in everything by prayer and supplication, with thanksgiving, let your requests be known to God; and the peace of God, which surpasses all understanding, will guard your hearts and minds through Christ Jesus.

—Philippians 4:6-7

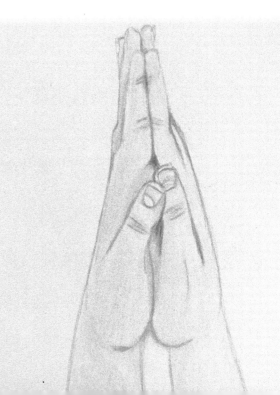

GET YOURSELF
STRAIGHTENED OUT FIRST, AND EVERYTHING ELSE WILL FALL INTO PLACE.

For where your treasure is, there your heart will be also.

—Matthew 6:21

DON'T WORRY ABOUT
WHAT'S BEHIND YOU. ALWAYS LOOK STRAIGHT AHEAD. BE READY FOR THE THINGS IN FRONT OF YOU.

In all your ways acknowledge Him, and He will direct your paths.

—Proverbs 3:6

KNOW WHO YOU ARE.

IF YOU DON'T, YOU MIGHT BELIEVE WHAT OTHERS TELL YOU THAT YOU ARE.

"No weapon forged against you will prevail, and you will refute every tongue that accuses you. This is the heritage of the servants of the Lord, and this is their vindication from me," declares the Lord.

—Isaiah 54:17

KNOW THAT YOU KNOW
THAT YOU KNOW.

For God so loved the world that He gave his one and only son that whosoever believes in Him shall not perish, but have everlasting life.

—John 3:16

Artwork by Whitney Herrington

YOU DON'T TELL
PEOPLE WHO YOU ARE.
YOU SHOW THEM.

But he gives us more grace. That is why Scripture says: God opposes the proud but shows favor to the humble.

—James 4:6

WHEN YOU GET OLDER,
YOU GOTTA ALWAYS WEAR A LITTLE RED. IT LETS PEOPLE KNOW YOU'RE STILL ALIVE.

Because of Christ and our faith in him, we can now come boldly and confidently into God's presence.

—Ephesians 3:12

THOSE WHO LOVE YOU . . .

LOVE YOU. THOSE WHO DON'T . . .

But I say to you who hear, Love your enemies, do good to those who hate you, bless those who curse you, pray for those who abuse you.

—Luke 6:27-28

IT CAN TAKE A LIFETIME

TO BUILD A REPUTATION BUT ONLY A SECOND TO KNOCK IT DOWN.

Anyone who listens to my teaching and follows it is wise, like a person who builds a house on solid rock. . . . But anyone who hears my teaching and doesn't obey it is foolish, like a person who builds a house on sand.

—Matthew 7:24-26

YOUR WALK TALKS
AND YOUR TALK TALKS, BUT YOUR WALK TALKS LOUDER THAN YOUR TALK TALKS.*

And this is love: that we walk in obedience to his commands. As you have heard from the beginning, his command is that you walk in love.

—2 John 1:6

* Quote attributed to John Maxewll

LOVE CHILDREN
AND THEY WILL LOVE YOU BACK.

Jesus said to them, "Let the little children come to me, and do not hinder them, for the kingdom of God belongs to such as these. Truly I tell you, anyone who will not receive the kingdom of God like a little child will never enter it." And he took the children in his arms, placed his hands on them and blessed them.

—Mark 10:13-16

IF YOU CAN HELP
ONE CHILD OR ONE PERSON BY
SHARING YOUR STORY—DO IT.

Jesus said, "Go home to your family, and tell them everything the Lord has done for you and how merciful he has been."

—Mark 5:19

YOU CAN'T FINISH
WHAT YOU NEVER STARTED.

I have fought the good fight, I have finished the race, I have kept the faith. Now there is in store for me the crown of righteousness, which the Lord, the righteous Judge, will award to me on that day—and not only to me, but also to all who have longed for his appearing.

—2 Timothy 4:7-8

**Culleoka FFA still reaps rewards
of longtime ag teachers' passion**

YOU NEVER SEE
AN ARMORED TRUCK
FOLLOWING A HEARSE.

The wicked borrow and do not repay, but the righteous give generously.

—Psalm 37:21

THAT'S THE BALLGAME
RIGHT THERE.

His master replied, "Well done, good and faithful servant! You have been faithful with a few things; I will put you in charge of many things. Come and share your master's happiness."

—Matthew 25:21

AN AFTERWORD
FROM THE FARMER'S DAUGHTER

As farmers sometimes say, "The hay is in the barn." The only thing left to do is bring out the hay, as needed.

Words that have been left on our hearts from special people are like that. Who has given you words of joy, hope, encouragement, comfort, guidance, laughter, or love?

Those are often the words that help us Cowboy Up in tough times, celebrate hard work that has been done, or help us leave our own legacy of life lessons behind.

Take a moment to write down, in the pages that follow, some of those words... words from your family, friends, or even these Hughisms that have been there just when you needed them.

And then, pass them on to others...who may need a little of the "hay" you've stored up in your life.

Blessings to Y'all,

— Regina

WORDS OF WISDOM AND LIFE STORED IN MY HEART

_____   _____
(NAME)   (DATE)